I YANKED WIGGLED AND PULLED BUT NOTHING WORKED

Way down south, just past the Gulf of Mexico, then beyond the coral reef, you will discover Greytail Ocean. A sea like no other. On this sparkling ocean floor is a shiny shark named Tootsie, who loves to play and explore.

GULF OF MEXICO

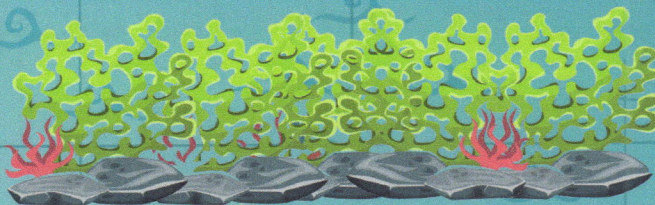

GRAYTAIL OCEAN

One day, as Tootsie stops to rest, she spots some sushi, and it's the best.

Tootsie takes a bite, but something just doesn't feel right.

Her tail brushes against the sandy carpet when she realizes she has found the toothy culprit; Tootsie has a loose tooth!

What is a shark supposed to do with a silly loose tooth, wondered Tootsie? I know I will go and see what Jake can do. He is, after all, the strongest octopus in the ocean. Thinks Tootsie. So, as fast as she could, Tootsie swam to the Coast to Go store and asked her friend Jake for help.

Jake tells Tootsie that he can help, "Tootsie, I will use my strength to yank your tooth out." But even though Jake yanked with all of his octopus might, Tootsie's tooth just would not come out.

A worried Tootsie swims faster than the Oceanic to find her friend, June the Jelly Fish, in hopes that June can help Tootsie out of this mess. Trying to help her friend, June wrapped her tentacles around Tootsie's tooth and wiggled as fast as she could.

But no matter how much she wiggled, Tootsie's tooth just would not come out.

Sea
Floss

Swimming around with a very loose tooth, Tootsie has no idea what she should do. When she saw her friend, Tommy the Turtle, who was busy flossing his teeth, Tommy told Tootsie that "I know what to do, I will use my Sea Floss to pull out your loose tooth."

Tommy pulled as hard as he could, but alas, Tootsie's tooth would not come out.

Sad, Tootsie swam around the ocean floor
wondering what she could do with her loose tooth.
When suddenly, Tootsie realized that she had just bumped
into Nancy the Narwhal.

Nancy asks Tootsie what was wrong, and so
Tootsie replied,

"Jake Yanked, June Wiggled, and Tommy Pulled,

but no matter what, nothing worked."

Can you help me, Nancy?

Nancy wonders to herself and then comes up with a plan.
Tootsie, I will use my magical horn to remove your tooth. So
Nancy placed her horn on Tootsie's tooth and said:
"toothy loosy wiggle and shake, turn this tooth into a cake."

Hurray!!!! Tootsie's tooth fell out, and it indeed did turn into a Bluetooth cake, and so Tootsie and all of her friends gathered to celebrate.

Contributing Authors

Little Authors

Contributing Authors

Landon Brown

Landon Brown is 7 years old and wants to be a Policeman when he grows up. He loves science, dinosaurs, and making Lego creations. He participates in soccer, basketball, little league baseball, and Cub Scouts. He is an avid reader and loves learning.

Michael Saxton

Michael R. Saxton is 10 years old and wants to be a Video game developer when he grows up. He loves to play video games, draw, watch people play games, and playing with animals. Michael is good at playing video games and has a passion for making and drawing video games.

Ian Miller

Ian Miller is 10 years old. He plays drums and aspires to be a rock star. He spends lots of time drawing and writing stories. Ian is a very fun-loving person who is always willing to help out.

LITTLE AUTHORS

CONTRIBUTING AUTHORS

LEVI BECERRA

BRODY BECERRA

MADISON HARBORTH

Levi Becerra is 8 years old and wants to be a Scientist when he grows up. He loves to play video games. Levi has a big heart and loves to help others.

Brody Becerra is 5 years old. He wants to be a Ninja when he grows up. He loves to go to the arcade. Brody is very excited to write this book and tell his story.

Madison Renae Hareborth is 6 years old, and she wants to be a Princess when she grows up! She loves to dress up and is all about fashion. She also enjoys writing and is very excited to be a part of this story. Madison is a fun-loving, energetic little girl and brings so much joy to all who are around her!

Little Authors

Contributing Authors

Lyndy Panter

My name is Lyndy, and I am 16 years old. I love to dance, sing, play piano, and I love to learn other languages. I want to be a school teacher when I'm older. I'm nice, and I bring everyone into the group. My goals are to become a great dancer, learner, and speak in a different language.

Caitlyn Saxton

Caitlyn E. Saxton is 14 years old and wants to be a Computer Programmer and Creative Writer when she grows up. She loves to read, write, paint, and sleep. Caitlyn has a soft spot for animals, and if she could, she would adopt every last one of them.

Lucy Miller

Lucy is 13 years old and has been writing stories for many years. She loves reading about severe weather occurrences and aspires to be a Meteorologist. She looks forward to writing many books in the future.

CECILIA MILLER

Cecilia Miller is 8 years old. She enjoys writing stories in her spare time. She wants to be a Musician when she grows up.

PEYTON HARBORTH

Peyton Rae Harborth is 7 years old. She loves playing all sports and being very active. She is very excited to be a part of this book and hopes her friends will enjoy reading it. Peyton is an awesome inventor and very creative!! She has the biggest heart and loves her family.

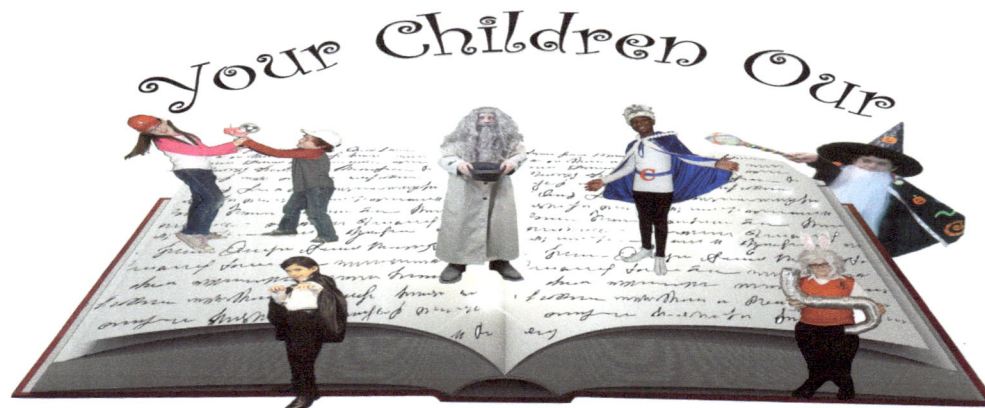

Your Children Our

Stories

CSB
INNOVATIONS

www.csbinnovations.com

www.ingramcontent.com/pod-product-compliance
Lightning Source LLC
Chambersburg PA
CBHW040406100426

42811CB00017B/1858